WHAT'S A WORDoodle?

WORDoodles is the new word craze that is sweeping across the country.
A WORDoodle is a very different way of looking at some common phrases.
This is a WORDoodle:

So is this:

STONE STONE STONE
STONE STONE STONE

The answer to the first one is "going around in circles," of course. The second one is a little harder. Try it for yourself. But remember—once you get started, you may not be able to stop.

WORDoodles

BY MARVIN MILLER

BANTAM BOOKS
NEW YORK / TORONTO / LONDON

To my wife, Matty,

    p
    u
    t

who s with things like this even
when they seem MAKE MAKE 0¢.*

*who puts up with things like this even when they seem to make no sense.

WORDoodles
A Bantam Book /
April 1980

All rights reserved.
Copyright © 1980 by Marvin Miller.
This book may not be reproduced in whole or in part, by
mimeograph or any other means, without permission.
For information address: Bantam Books, Inc.

ISBN 0-553-13905-3

Published simultaneously in the United States and Canada

Bantam Books are published by Bantam Books, Inc. Its trademark, consisting of the words "Bantam Books" and the portrayal of a bantam, is Registered in U.S. Patent and Trademark Office and in other countries. Marca Registrada. Bantam Books, Inc., 666 Fifth Avenue, New York, New York 10019.

PRINTED IN THE UNITED STATES OF AMERICA

0 9 8 7 6 5 4 3 2 1

INTRODUCTION

How wise of you to read this introduction first! Resisting the temptation to solve a few quick WORDoodles says alot about you. I promise your patience will be rewarded.

As you quickly have guessed, WORDoodles are common words or phrases expressed in a different way. They just sit there staring up at you (or down, depending upon your reading position) and try to say something very familiar in a strange but clever way. Don't try to pronounce them. Like the old adage, most WORDoodles are meant to be seen and not heard.

Let's start by getting the feel for a WORDoodle. Try your hand at number one. After you think you know each one (or even if you don't), turn to the clue section (page 60) for help or confirmation. Then when you're really sure, check the answer (page 62). No need to hurry with this. I'll wait here until you're finished.

. . . That was pretty good for a beginner. Now you've got the hang of it. You have already noted that WORDoodles can become habit forming and, as you will see, knowing their answer can often be as much fun as figuring out the WORDoodle itself.

Even if you think you know the solution, check the clue section to verify your hunch. Use either as a thermometer or like a crib sheet — to check your feelings, or to help you see the answer in a different light.

Below is a sampling of the different types of WORDoodles you are likely to come across. It might be a good idea to try the WORDoodle after reading each description:

WORDoodle
NUMBER

- 2B WORDoodle indicating size
- 2C WORDoodle indicating direction or position
- 3A WORDoodle with a simple line or symbol
- 3B WORDoodle that makes use of the letters within it
- 3C WORDoodle signifying action
- 4A WORDoodle using words that have a meaning in another sense

Finished? See, you are getting better already. Definitely out of the amateur class. The more WORDoodles you do, the easier they become to solve.

Now here are a few tips to help you on the road to becoming a master WORDoodler:

- Look at the WORDoodle and try to get the feeling of what it is trying to say. More often than not you'll go astray if you try to pronounce it.
- Look at the letters, the words and the way they are assembled. Check to make sure the spelling is correct.
- Since WORDoodles are a kind of shorthand, add words like "and" or "the" where they make sense. Don't overlook a squiggle or strangely appearing letter. Give the editor some credit. He is only trying to help.
- As mentioned above, be sure to use the clue section as a stopping-off place. Persons solving crossword puzzles with a ballpoint pen can disregard this tip.

While I doubt that WORDoodles will replace speedwriting or achieve literary prominence, I hope this book spawns a cult of WORDoodles addicts. But most of all, I hope you will share your favorites with friends — like a charming poem or witty cartoon. And like that cartoon, a good WORDoodle is worth a thousand words!

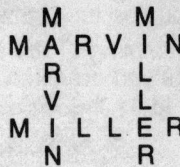

WORDoodles 1

S̸T̸A̸M̸P̸

a. _____

CYCLE
CYCLE
CYCLE

b. _____

GREENNV

c.

2

GOING GOING GOING GOING GOING GOING GOING GOING GOING GOING

a.
___

JOHN JOHN

b.
___

L C
L U
U R
P B

c.

3

LOOK ME EYE

a. _____

GUYYY

b. _____

PROM   ISE

c.

4

10 J Q K A
FACTS

a. _____

M U S I C

b. _____

STONE STONE STONE STONE STONE STONE

c.

Y-O-U-N-G M-A-N

a. _____

1900

b. _____

DO ft. OR

c.

6

$$\frac{GO}{JAN\ 6\ \ FEB\ 3}$$

a.
___

$$\frac{O}{\begin{array}{c}MD\\DDS\\BS\end{array}}$$

b.
___

c.

7

LOOK KOOL CROSSING

a. _____

PERFORM A^+ NCE

b. _____

ONE ANOTHER
ONE ANOTHER
ONE ANOTHER
ONE ANOTHER
ONE ANOTHER
ONE ANOTHER

c.

8

FTORREESST

a. _____

POTOOOOOOOO

b. _____

R/E/A/D/I/N/G

c.

PANTANTANTS

a.

PLAY
PLAY

C
C
I
H

b.   c.

R A C K

d.

10

SIDK DKIS

a. _____

$$\frac{\text{TAKE}}{\text{JOB}}$$

b. _____

STA TION

c.

11

GETIT

a. _____

$$8-6=2$$

b. _____

FEET

c. _____

MI LES

d.

12

BLOOD WATER

a. _____

$$\mathbf{I \atop T}$$

b. _____

NOW ^HE~RE~

c.

13

HIS·TORY

a. _____

COLLAR

b. _____

THROAT

c.

14

L ME RI K Y

a. _____

b. _____

JOYFU

c.

15

$$\frac{21\text{ lb}}{\text{HAND}} \quad \frac{18\text{ lb}}{\text{FOOT}}$$

a.

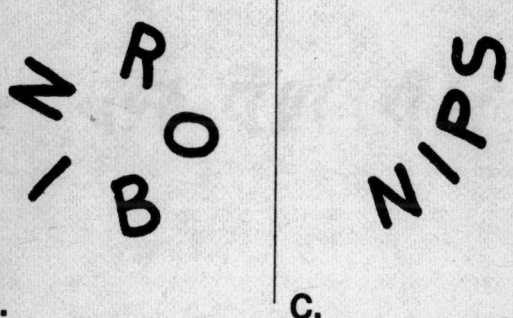

b.   c.

ESGG GESG

d.

16

TABLE TABLE

a.
___

פֿאַ פֿאַ פֿאַ

b.
___

$$\frac{I}{8}$$

c.

17

JUDGMENT

a. _____

WHEATHER

b. _____

CHEEK CHEEK

c.

18

PAR / FEELING

a. _____

PLAYING

b. _____

1935 1962 ALONG 1973

c.

19

$$\frac{\text{IT IT}}{\text{AGAIN}}$$

a.

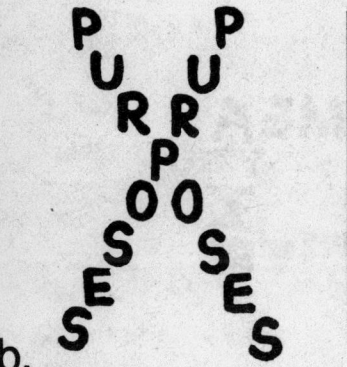

b.   c.

$$\frac{\text{HE}}{\text{BACKWARDS}}$$

d.

20

ƎlddA∃NId CAKE

a. _____

MEAL / ALME / LMEA / EALM (square)

b. _____

PUBLIC + DRESS

c.

21

$$\frac{T E S}{\text{THINGS}}$$

a. _____

U (O) ME

b. _____

NOITAN

c.

22

$$\frac{ii}{oo} \frac{ii}{oo}$$

a. _____

FR1DAY 5ATURDAY

b. _____

P_pO_pD

c.

23

TRAPPED

a. _____

SUIT
SIT
IT
T

b. _____

TIME TIME

c.

24

$$\frac{\text{PAID}}{\text{ONE}} \quad \frac{\text{PAID}}{\text{WON}} \quad \frac{\text{PAID}}{1}$$

a. _____

2222DAY

b. _____

TIITH

c.

 ✓✓ ✓
COUNTER

a. ____________________

PANTS
PANTS

b. ____________________

ECNALG

c.

26

FvOaRlMuAaTbIlOeN

a. _____

VVIISSIIOONN

b. _____

KNOW IT TI

c.

27

EILN PU

a. _____

$$\text{L}^A_{WY}ER$$

b. _____

EVER EVER EVER EVER MONDAY

c.

28

$$\frac{\text{MMAG}}{\text{BOARD}}$$

a. _____

b. _____

DAYS DAYS DAYS DAYS DAYS

c.

29

FRU BID BID BID BID IT

a. _____

b. _____

$$\frac{STOP}{10¢}$$

c.

30

$$5/0 \quad 5/0$$

a. _____

$$N^A T^I O N$$

b. _____

$$\frac{\text{GROUND}}{\begin{array}{c}\text{FEET}\\\text{FEET}\\\text{FEET}\\\text{FEET}\\\text{FEET}\\\text{FEET}\end{array}}$$

c.

31

RODO LBLE

a. _____

WAETURNINGRTS (inverted)

b. _____

LIP
LIP (mirrored)

c.

32

DICTNRY

a. _____

BBRIDE

b. _____

OPEEEN

c.

33

CREAM

a. _____

GET DOGGIE

b. _____

P
O
P
P STOP

c.

34

MEAL ONE
MEAL ONE
MEAL ONE

a. _____

HOURS KEEP WORKING

b. _____

EXCITING MR. E

c.

35

PUIBLC

a. _____

YO R COUNTRY

b. _____

BAN   ANA

c.

36

a. GNIPEEK SESENOJ

b. OPEN MMMM

c. OFOFOFOFOF OF OFOFOFOF

37

BED T
     E
    G

a. _____

1,001,000

b. _____

HE
HE / HIMSELF
HE

c.

38

GOWN

a. _____

END | 25 PENNIES
    | 5 NICKLES
    | 1 QUARTER

b. _____ c.

VIRGO
....

d.

HAND M
E

a. _____

b. _____

COUNNNNTRY

c.

40

TE ETH

a. _____

oArPaPnLgEeSs

b. _____

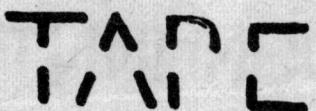

c.

41

STATES

a.
___

EVERY RIGHT THING

b.
___

THINGS

c.

42

C O D C T
C N U U

a. _____

HURRIEDLY

b. _____

DUTCH D$_W$D$_E$D$_S$D$_T$D

c.

$$1,2,3,4,\overset{5}{\cancel{6}},6,7,8,9$$

a. _____

CECRET

b. _____

$A¢K$

c.

44

~~WATERGATE~~

a.
___

[[[[[[[[[[

b.
___

MIRROR (mirrored)

c.

SLEEVE

a.
___

ALL 1111 AND 1 ALL ALL ALL ALL

b.
___

RYT YTR TRY TYR RTY YRT

c.

46

ROAT

a. _____

CRUST (upside down)   **Oo**

b. _____ | c.

STICk

d.

47

OMPANY

a. _____

PHOTOGRAPH

b. _____

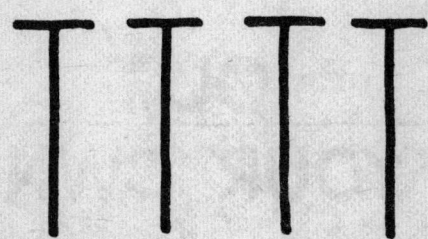

c.

48

1NFLAT1ON

a. _____

HIGH WAY

b. _____

~~ØUT~~
YOUR OWN

c.

49

JANUA

a. _____

MAILZBOX

b. _____

BBBBROOK

c.

50

llobbster

a. _____

SUPERBOWL

b. _____

HAHAHA sHAdow

c.

51

$$\frac{\text{EADY}}{\text{TIME}}$$

a. _____

STREET TSERTS

b. _____

c.

52

ARRIVE TIME

a.

M M
A A
R R
T T
I I
N N
I I

b.

c.

TOE SOFTLY

a.

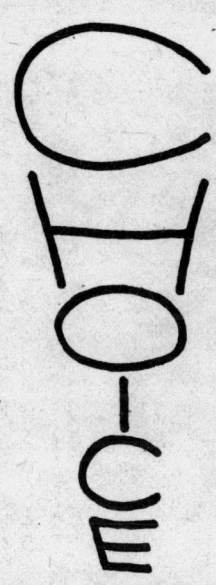

b.

c.

CLUES

1
- A Postal work
- B Kiddie carrier
- C Color me jealous

2
- A Dizzy activity
- B Close, warm feeling
- C Cop call

3
- A Lie detector
- B Smart aleck
- C In default

4
- A Demand information
- B Punk rock
- C Immaculate beachcomber

5
- A Handsome fellow
- B 100-year wait
- C Salesman's shoehorn

6
- A Foursome fun
- B Ice cold
- C Sorry about that

7
- A Safety first
- B Smashing review
- C It's all the same to me

8
- A Shortsighted lumberjack
- B In the chips
- C More than meets the eye

9
- A Fidgety flannels
- B Going out together
- C Excuse me
- D Behind the line

10
- A Need straightening out
- B Sizable stint
- C Time for a commercial

11
- A Become level-headed
- B Half of the remainder
- C Two policemen
- D Far away

12
- A It runs in the family
- B All inclusive
- C Man from Atlantis

13
- A Stone Age
- B Fatherly appearance
- C Adam's apple

14
- A Some like it warm
- B Novelette
- C Christmas greeting

15
- A Exceptional service
- B Mixed play
- C Garden grown
- D Yolk for mixed company

16
- A Reverse the situation
- B In need of plastic surgery
- C Weight Watcher candidate

17
- A Quick decision
- B It rained for days
- C Neck twister

18
- A Icky all over
- B Eligible receiver
- C Age marches on

19
- A What did you say?
- B Clashing activity
- C Angry feeling
- D Special effort

20
- A On the roof of the mouth
- B Hearty portions
- C Four score and ...

21
- A Small annoyance
- B Not even a smidgen
- C Wishful thinking

22
- A Insomniac
- B Omen
- C Double bed

23
- A When to climb the walls
- B Perfect fit
- C Incentive wages

24
- A Shortchanged
- B 3/7
- C Watch your diet

25
- A Pay before leaving
- B Hip huggers
- C Rear vision

CLUES

26
A Important material
B Get a second look
C A to Z and Z to A

27
A I comes after e
B Shady tricks
C Eternity + 1

28
A 30 pieces to play with
B Deep water
C Series of 24 hours

29
A Do not touch
B Time will tell
C Screeching halt

30
A Dutch treat
B Neutral soil
C Pushing daisies

31
A Knock before entering
B Reverse gears
C Face with courage

32
A At a loss for words
B Gentleman's agreement
C Flip-top can

33
A A base to make-up
B Texas dachsund
C Infield out

34
A Just what the doctor ordered
B How to get WORDoodle 23 C
C Hair-raising Hitchcock

35
A Let's be more discreet
B Message from Uncle Sam
C Lots of calories

36
A Match game
B Coliseum
C Again and again

37
A Grouchy riser
B 999,999 are the same
C In a dither

38
A How to get a chest cold
B Source of boxtops
C Read Thomas Paine
D End of an agreement

39
A Oldies but goodies
B Almost too late
C Overseas location

40
A Orthodontist's delight
B Illogical reasoning
C Temporary cover-up

41
A Fabulous fifty
B Surrounded
C Bright outlook

42
A Court trouble
B Speedy exit
C Aruba and environs

43
A No comment
B Classified
C Brinks bags

44
A Cleaning after the plumbers
B Copycat correspondent
C Backward reflection

45
A Cardshark apparel
B United we stand
C Make every effort

46
A On the level
B High Society
C A fine state
D Worst part to grab

47
A Adios
B No color at all
C Annoying pest

48
A Dollar shrinker
B Do not pass
C You'd rather do it yourself

49
A 1/1/80 1/1/81 1/1/82
B Drop a line
C Mumbling water

50
A Scaled seafood
B What Conference winners do
C Cranston's snicker

CLUES

51
A. A few minutes late
B. WORDoodle 7A is good advice
C. Long shot

52
A. Pop in early
B. Stiff order
C. Keeping the budget balanced

53
A. Shhh
B. Process of elimination
C. Cut short

ANSWERS

1
A. Cancelled stamp
B. Tricycle
C. Green with envy

2
A. Going around in circles
B. Long johns
C. Pull up along side the curb

3
A. Look me square in the eye
B. Wise guy
C. Broken promise

4
A. Hand over the facts
B. Spaced-out music
C. No stone unturned

5
A. Dashing young man
B. Turn of the century
C. Put a foot in the door

6
A. Go on a double date
B. Three degrees below zero
C. Excuse me

7
A. Look both ways before crossing
B. High-grade performance
C. Six of one, half dozen of another

8
A. Can't see the forest for the trees
B. Potatoes
C. Reading between the lines

9
A. Ants in the pants
B. Double play
C. Hiccup
D. Halfback

10
A. Mixed up kids
B. Take on a big job
C. Station break

11
A. Get it all together
B. Split the difference
C. Flat feet
D. Miles apart

12
A. Blood is thicker than water
B. The long and short of it
C. He came out of nowhere

13
A. A period in history
B. Turned up collar
C. Lump in the throat

14
A. Lime Rickey without ice
B. Cut a long story short
C. Joyful Noel

15
A. Wait on hand and foot
B. Round robin
C. Turnips
D. Two scrambled eggs

16
A. Turn the tables
B. Nose all bent out of shape
C. I overate

ANSWERS

17
A Snap judgment
B A terrible spell of weather
C Turn the other cheek

18
A Feeling below par
B Playing tight end
C Along in years

19
A Repeat it over again
B Cross purposes
C Rub the wrong way
D He leaned over backwards

20
A Pineapple upside-down cake
B Three square meals
C Public address

21
A Upset over little things
B There is nothing between you and me
C Half a notion

22
A Circles under the eyes
B Days are numbered
C Two peas in a pod

23
A Trapped in a corner
B Suit to a T
C Time and a half

24
A Everyone is underpaid
B Tuesday
C Eyeteeth

25
A Checkout counter
B Pair of pants
C Backward glance

26
A Valuable information
B Double vision
C Know it backwards and forwards

27
A Line up in alphabetical order
B Crooked lawyer
C Forever and a day

28
A Backgammon board
B Hole at the bottom of the sea
C Days on end

29
A Forbidden fruit
B It remains to be seen
C Stop on a dime

30
A Fifty-fifty split
B Nonaligned nation
C Six feet under ground

31
A Doorbell out of order
B Turning around in midstream
C Stiff upper lip

32
A Abridged dictionary
B Bride-to-be
C Open with ease

33
A Vanishing cream
B Get along little doggie
C Pop-up by the shortstop

34
A One after every meal
B Keep working after hours
C Exciting mystery

35
A You and I should not be together in public
B Your country needs you
C Banana Split

36
A Keeping up with the Joneses
B Open forum
C Often times

37
A Get up on the wrong side of bed
B One in a million
C He's beside himself

38
A Low-cut gown
B Open end
C Common sense
D Sign on the dotted line

39
A Hand-me-down
B Nick of time
C Foreign country

ANSWERS

40
A Space between the teeth
B Mixing apples and oranges
C Masking tape

41
A United States
B Right in the middle of everything
C Things are starting to look better

42
A Disorderly conduct
B Hurriedly departed
C Dutch West Indies

43
A Fifth Amendment
B Top secret
C Sacks of money

44
A Watergate cover-up
B Chain letter
C Rearview mirror

45
A Ace up the sleeve
B All for one and one for all
C Try every which way

46
A Flat bottom boat
B Upper crust
C Ohio
D Short end of the stick

47
A Part company
B Black and white photograph
C Big tease

48
A Double digit inflation
B Divided highway
C Strike out on your own

49
A Beginning of January
B Put a letter in the mailbox
C Babbling brook

50
A 2 lb. lobster
B Finish up in the Super Bowl
C The Shadow has the last laugh

51
A Almost ready on time
B Two-way street
C Fat chance

52
A Arrive ahead of time
B Double Martini straight up with a twist
C Cutting corners to make ends meet

53
A Tiptoe softly
B Narrow down the choice
C Nip in the bud